Undone to Well Done

A Quick and Painless Self Help Guide to Finishing Your Master's or Doctorate Degree

V.S. Chochezi

ISBN: 9798840218945

LIVECATION

Long live the knowledge seekers, the scholars of ancient Timbuktu, the writers, the knowers and the seers. This simple guide is created with the energy of the Green Book, the spirit of Mary McCleoud Bethune, the fortitude of George Washington Carver, the respect for Shirley Graham Du Bois and Dr. W.E.B. Du Bois, and the heart of the Little Rock 9.

CONTENTS

ACKNOWLEDGMENTS

Merci beaucoup, muchas gracias, asante sana, much thanks and appreciation to all those who supported me on my own advanced degree journeys and the writing, editing and publishing of this guide. Umoja - Unity is one of my guiding principles. It is seriously easier said than done , but is something for which I strive . I recognize that time working on an advanced degree was time away from my family, but saw it as an investment in a brighter future for all of us. So, first I must thank my very best friend, biggest fan, my birth mother, first mother and an amazing woman like no other, Staajabu. Staajabu goaded me into writing the book and helped me squash the negative Nellie in my head that thought of every excuse to throw roadblocks and self-doubts in my path. Though she holds zero degrees, she has supported many along the path to degree completion whether undergraduate, law, medical, or other advanced degrees. She is the real MVP (most valuable player), the best dissertation coach, and she deserves an honorary doctorate for her many contributions to society. Thank you mom! Big kudos to my daughters Jessicah and Tisho and my grandchildren who carried on while I worked to provide and studied to elevate our situations. Thank you to my late father, to my step moms, sisters, brother/s, nieces, nephews, aunties, uncles, and cousins for all of your continued positive vibrations and well wishes. My family has been very motivating, intentionally or otherwise. I was taught that we are here to serve and to share our gifts. This product is an effort to continue that practice. Your support will help in the endeavor.

Thank you to Historically Black Colleges and Universities, especially Delaware State University, and Howard University which were critically important to my successes. Thank you to my former professors throughout all of my academic pursuits, and especially to Drexel University which propelled my thoughts, ideas and skill levels forward tremendously. Thank you to all who aided me directly in my pursuit of the doctoral degree including Dr. Angelo Williams, the late honorable James Sweeney, Dr. Carl Mack, my entire Drexel Sacramento cohort 1, and all those who I may be forgetting in this moment, but for whom I'm no less grateful.

Lastly, thank you dear reader. My sincere hope is that this product helps you and/or someone you love.

Peace! Salaam! Amani! Paz! Paix!

1 PROLOG

Cross the finish Line no matter where you stopped.

Get unstuck. Finish your advanced degree.

Go from all but the comprehensive exams, All But the Dissertation (ABD) or All but the thesis to being awarded the master's or doctorate degree

Feeling stuck, like a failure, devastated?

Speaking to people who either started yet never finished the advanced degree themselves, or who know someone in this category, the stories of anguish, agony, lingering feelings of utter failure and lasting shame are tremendous. The full extent of how many people pay for and complete all of the required coursework on the path to the master's and doctoral degrees, but never complete the thesis, culminating requirements or dissertation and thus leave the academy absent the degree remains seriously underreported and less than fully analyzed.

In a 2014 article by Rebecca Shuman, published in *Slate* magazine, she stated that the 10-year completion rate for Ph. Ds after beginning studies in humanities was at 49 percent. The highest completion rates were in STEM at 55-64 percent (Shuman 2014). This equates to a whole lot of incomplete doctoral degrees, and it is doubtful that those numbers have improved through the years.

I came to focus on this topic when I went through my own master's journey, entering a two-year program of study. I quickly realized that the course offerings and the overall program centered around full-time students and as a working single mom, and part-time student, the finish line would take me possibly twice as long to reach. During my first two years, living in Sacramento, I met people all over the region with painful stories of acing the coursework, getting through exams, completing the thesis or dissertation proposal of two to three approved chapters out of five needed to complete the process, but never successfully finishing the degree. It was a very terrifying and depressing foreboding to consider that this could also be my fate. I vowed that I would not give up and would succeed in earning my degree. It took me a full seven years to obtain the master's degree when I anticipated that it would take me four to five years going part-time. I have vowed to help others avoid the common pitfalls that derail us in our pursuit of attaining advanced degrees. I have been assisting individuals through the process for many years. My biggest fan, my mom, Staajabu began encouraging me to capture my ideas around the topic into a book to potentially help more people. Thus, this publication was born.

2 ADVANCED DEGREE JOURNEY

As an east coast transplant, my first introduction to California community colleges was working at one as a liberal arts department secretary in the Bay area, back when secretarial positions were still en vogue. I was impressed with California community colleges! I had attended Historically Black Colleges and Universities on the east coast and had earned a bachelor's degree in journalism. I was a single mother with two small children living in Oakland, CA and struggling to pay rent, childcare, transportation costs and other bills to stay afloat. I had interned in alumni affairs and pursued a career in that area after graduation, but wasn't landing entry level positions in the field on par with my degree and experience. Though I was underemployed in the secretarial position, it allowed me to work on a nice campus, included paid benefits and seemed like a steppingstone to something better, though I really didn't know all that I would learn. I was underemployed because the secretary position didn't require a bachelor's degree, but the degree is what made me more competitive than many of the other applicants and gave me an edge to get the job.

Having gone right from high school to a four year degree granting institution on the east coast, I didn't know anything really about community colleges. There seemed to be a bit of a negative stigma about attending and working at community colleges. The thinking among my peers seemed to be that community colleges were a stepping stone to something better.

Working at the community college was enlightening and inspirational. As the department secretary, I interacted with students, faculty, staff and administrators daily. The professors seemed to enjoy their jobs with a passion. They made the work look fun and rewarding. I asked a lot of questions. This is when and where I decided to pursue a career as a California community college instructor. The first step, I was informed, was to get a master's degree.

This didn't seem like a hurdle since I had graduated cum laude with a bachelor's degree. Soon enough, I was admitted into a master's program. The program was advertised as a two year program. It was not set up for working professionals. It was geared toward full-time students who could take courses during the day. Though I left the secretarial job and relocated, I was able to find full-time employment though again, not employment that required a bachelor's degree, so while I was getting good benefits (medical, dental, paid sick leave and vacation days) I was underemployed, making low wages and struggling to keep all the bills paid.I was able to work with employers and the college to flex my schedule and take fewer classes each semester and finished the course work in about three or four years. I was also fortunate to participate in a faculty internship and to work as a graduate teaching assistant. The work was enjoyable. I respected my professors, appreciated my peers, and relished student interactions.

Once entering the graduate program, I was very concerned that wherever I went around town, when I would tell people about the master's program, I would meet many people (mostly Black people) who had gone through the program, finished the coursework, but never completed the degree. I vowed that would not be my fate. With a bachelor's degree in journalism and nearly straight As in the master's courses, I thought myself a strong writer and believed that writing a thesis would be challenging, but readily achievable. In the end, it took me the full seven years, and I did eventually earn the master's degree. It was indeed challenging, but not in the ways I had anticipated. I learned a great deal navigating a majority dominant culture university as a Black woman, and committed myself to help others, especially from marginalized groups, do the same. I am still assisting people who have completed most of the requirements for the master's degree, as well as for doctoral programs, but who have stalled and given up on ever finishing and actually receiving the degree by getting through the comprehensive exams, thesis process, Institutional Review Board (IRB) and dissertation processes.

Each person's situation is different. Each advanced degree journey is unique. There are specific thesis and dissertation review committees to navigate. There are various processes and formats required for each. There is no one-size fits all approach to completing the process. However, if you are in the position of ABD, or all but the thesis for the master's degree, this publication is meant to give you encouragement and some guidance on how to get back on track to reclaim and achieve your goal of earning the advanced degree.

Obtaining a master's or doctoral degree creates many opportunities not necessarily available to you without it, especially if your passion is to teach or in higher education administration.

3 GRADUATE PROGRAMS ARE COLLABORATIVE

Undergraduate practices don't transfer smoothly for Graduate studies

One area that many of us who are the first in our families to pursue advanced degrees fail to understand about master's and doctoral programs is the relationship building part. Many of us attend commuter schools in our undergraduate studies. We work, raise our families and chunk out our education part time over many years. Even when we attend full-time, we generally have little time for extra-curricular school related activities, instead rushing from class to work, or to attend to family obligations. We bond with only a few professors and classmates beyond time spent with them in the classroom. Too often, we expect these same tactics that served us adequately in our undergraduate studies, to work in graduate school as well.

The coursework is still important in graduate school. The importance of relationships and networking increases in graduate school. It becomes critically important to have advisors, thesis and dissertation committee members who are either passionate about your area of study and/or invested in your well-being as an individual. They should be aware of you as a holistic human being, and not just as a graduate student. It is also very beneficial for you to know your advisors and committee members on a more personal level. Read their scholarship and know their interests, hobbies, and pet peeves, preferably before enrolling into a program of study. Understand that your thesis and dissertation reflect on them as well. They have to sign off on it. It is truly a collaboration, so give and take is an important part of the process.

4 SANKOFA MOMENTS

Now, let me share with you what I call "Sankofa moments". In my twenties, I was vested in a public service job, and when I left the job, I cashed out my retirement. It was a painful lesson as they took at least 50% of the money in my account for taxes, and then penalized me for early withdrawal. So, what looked like a nice chunk of change ended up just being a little bit of play money. It felt good in the moment, but I quickly came to second guess and somewhat regret that move. I cashed out approximately $13,000 and ended up with maybe $5,000 after taxes and penalties. I beat myself up for years over it. Then, five years ago, I was able to take retirement savings from the next job and transfer it back into that account to buy back that time that I had recklessly cashed out in my youth. The buy back cost more than $40,000. I am still learning how that will serve me in the future. I have been blessed to experience many second chances and to beat myself up less over hard choices and to be more hopeful and confident that things will work out for the best in the end if I trust my instincts, stay diligent and put in the work.

One of my missions that is continuing to grow is to be somewhat of a thesis/dissertation coach and/or consultant. In prepping for my pep talk to one of my mentees, I began thinking about this idea that may help others here and of course is helpful to me as well.

Sankofa lesson one comes from the experience of withdrawing my retirement savings early, then buying the investment back later.

Sankofa lesson 1: It's not too late. One interpretation of Sankofa is that it means go back and fetch it. Whatever that thing that you feel you left undone in the past, seize the moment now. Fix it.

Sankofa lesson two stems from another example with student loans. It's true. I have a master's degree and a doctorate degree. I also owe a LOT of money in student loans. Possibly through no fault of my own, I'm learning, I missed out on getting loan forgiveness. I knew I should be eligible. I worked in public service for decades, but I didn't get eligible for loan forgiveness until four years ago. Well, if you owe student loans, and if you have been paying attention, there is a window open now where you can go back and claim that time going back as far as 2007. Yes, it can be excruciating paperwork and phone calls and staying on top of the various agencies and organizations, but I believe it will result in much of my loans being forgiven before I retire or expire.

Sankofa lesson two: What seems challenging or like a mistake in one moment could turn around and work out fine later in life. Try not to fall apart, lose confidence or wallow in regret for long. Trust your instincts.

Because I know some of you need more convincing, I will share one more Sankofa example. I bought my house in 2006. It was supposed to be a starter house, not my dream home. My realtor believed that in two or three years, the house would appreciate greatly and I could take the equity and buy my dream home. But then the market crashed in 2008 and a $175,000 house depreciated to be worth only $70,000. This was not ideal, but still manageable, until I was laid off in 2011. And, I began to second guess my choice and feel like I had made a big mistake in buying a house. However, after MANY phone calls and MUCH paperwork to modify my loan and get it down to manageable payments, now, houses are appreciating and equity is building once again. I still don't have my dream home, but I've been able to make many improvements and make it much more comfortable for myself in my current house, for which I am very grateful.

Sankofa lesson three: Try again!

If you left without the degree and you still want that degree, what will it really hurt to begin to do the research and begin the process of being reinstated?

Get back in there and finish it Sankofa!! You can do it!! If you left something undone in the past, go back and get it! Don't be embarrassed to ask for what you want. Let them tell you no. Then, ask again. Ask someone else; ask in a different way; be persistent; enlist help; but don't stop at no and don't stop until you get what you already more than halfway completed. Really, you are more than halfway finished already. So, if you are ready to get back in, or if you are considering a master's or a doctoral program for the first time, take in the following information. This publication is for you.

5 PICK THE RIGHT PROGRAM

Choosing the right program for you will set you up for success from the outset. Consider what will work best for you. Identify cost, online or in-person instruction, day or evening class availability, faculty and staff expertise and compatibility, mentoring availability, graduation rates and reports on what program graduates do upon degree completion.

After being admitted into the program, network and begin to strategize about your thesis/project or dissertation committee. Ideally, your committee members, and especially your chairperson will be excited to work with you on your topic, and they will be approachable and available when you have questions and concerns.

Some wonder about whether to pursue the Ph.D. or the Ed.D. There is no right or wrong choice. Many factors will determine the best path for your needs. Be certain to consider what you wish to do with the degree. If you are pursuing a full-time tenured faculty position at a research institution, the Ph.D. may be the way to go. If you wish to become an administrator in the community college system or public state universities, the Ed.D might be a good option. Other factors to consider include whether you plan to conduct active field research which is typically the realm of the Ed.D. or whether you intend to focus on philosophical and more theoretical material, typically the concentration for Ph.D. dissertation work.

Overcome hurdles

If you encounter hardships, setbacks, writer's block, or other issues that may derail your progress, don't ignore it. Seek help. Don't let issues linger. Recommit and focus. If your committee isn't working out, consider changing committee members. Many programs will allow you to pick at least one person outside your department. Sometimes you can even select a committee member from another college. Sometimes this change is enough to set you back on the right path.

You need cheerleaders

Assemble your team of cheerleaders. Often family and friends will not understand or be particularly supportive of the time you will need to devote to your studies, research and writing to complete an advanced degree. Cohort models have shown great results. If your program doesn't follow a cohort structure, consider forming unofficial study groups and social break groups where you can get together at least once a month for a few hours to unwind.

6 GET REINSTATED

If you have labored to get a master's or a doctorate and finished almost everything, but just couldn't get past the exams, project or the thesis or dissertation phase, maybe it is not too late. Consider enlisting a dissertation coach, or graduate degree coach.

Never be too embarrassed to seek extra help as soon as you recognize that you are struggling and stalling. Avoid imposter syndrome. Maintain confidence. You had what it takes to be admitted into the program. You are good enough. You can do it, and you are needed among the ranks of college faculty and administration. If you were in a master's program or a doctoral program and it didn't work out, consider asking for a review and reinstatement, explaining the circumstances that led to your premature departure. If they say no, appeal. Now may be the right time for you to jump back in and finish.

Sometimes there has been a change of faculty while you were on pause from your degree pursuit. Though working with a team who is familiar with your work may seem the best route, new committee members may give you an opportunity for a fresh start. Working with a new member may be an opportunity to work with someone who is more supportive of your goal to finish the degree.

Tips for requesting reinstatement

Here are some handy helpful tips for when you speak to or meet with individuals about reinstatement into the master's/doctoral program:

1. Be clear about what you want as the outcome. Identify what you want done. It helps if you can write it out. It's extra helpful if you can say it in a couple of sentences. For example, do you want to be reinstated by a certain date, without additional coursework? Do you want specialized staff support with a detailed timeline and an expected completion date? Understand the cost of reinstatement and the payment structure expected upon readmittance.

2. Be clear what compromises/concessions you are willing to accept, whether you decide to share the ideas or not.

3. If the people you are meeting with/reaching out to can't supply what you want, probe to see if they can they point you in the right direction.

4. Write down your questions before the meeting so if you get side tracked, you get all your questions answered and if you run out of time, you can send the unanswered questions in an email.

Not sure where to begin? If your previous advisor is still around, it is probably a good idea to start there. Each institution is different, and the process may differ widely based on the department. Other places to consider starting include the office of graduate studies, and you also may be able to enlist help from alumni affairs. Use the internet to help guide you in terms of determining specific individuals to contact, via phone and/or email.

Request for Reinstatement

Many programs have information online about how to be reinstated. The processes vary. Some are well developed and fairly specific. Others are more general and will require more research to pin down. Be brave! The worst case scenario is that they say no, you can't be reinstated and you have to reapply and start over from scratch. This is when you will weigh whether you want to give the institution that let you down and is now being completely unhelpful, more of your hard earned money, or if you want to start over with a new, better, more supportive institution.

7 SELF CARE

Graduate school is hard. It is meant to be hard. Push yourself. Sometimes you will get tired and want to just quit. Remember that you are capable. You can do this. Don't give up on yourself, but breaks are allowed. Build time into your weekly schedule for self care. Practice journaling, meditating, yoga, taking walks outside and focusing on breathing, going to the gym, talking to friends and loved ones to just touch base and catch up, try doodling, painting, drawing, singing, cooking, sewing, knitting, crocheting, fishing or any other activity that feeds your spirit and gives your mind a break from your studies periodically. The breaks should sustain you and allow you to push forward when needed. However, remember that your priority is to finish the degree. Don't allow yourself to get distracted for long. There will be time for play and leisure after the degree is complete.

8 TESTIMONIES

I have helped dozens of people complete their graduate degree journey successfully. Following are just a few testimonies from those I've assisted.

Testimony 1:

VS Chochezi has been an intricate part in me continuing to push forward in completing my doctorate program. Through her support and knowledge of the process, I was able to write an appeal to the Ph.D. Board and get reinstated after six years of leaving the program without completing the degree. She continues to help in supporting me through the use of check-in's and providing any assistance necessary to ensure that I will be successful at completing this next phase of my life. (Tamu L.)

Testimony 2:

Dr. Chochezi was an inspiration to me on my dissertation journey. First, it was the way she entered her program, there was no fanfare, no long discussions of should I or shouldn't I, just I'm going to do it. And then there she was, in it!! Working full time, still doing poetry and other advocacy events around Sacramento, taking classes, studying and dreaming up her dissertation project. This too was inspiring to me, the lack of drama, angst, or self-pity, just focus and determination. What also impressed me deeply was Dr. Chochezi's deep commitment to service after graduation. This degree was not for her but for the community. She continued her program through the great recession, being laid off, having health issues, steadily putting one foot in front of the other, staying inspired throughout. I didn't know I was going to pursue a PhD at that time, didn't even consider it, but when the opportunity presented itself, I remembered how she did it and said, "Why not?" and just dived right in! When challenges arose, I whined, moaned and complained. She listened. Sometimes giving the perfect advice and sometimes simply listening. Those were the days I wasn't ready for advice and needed compassionate mentorship and encouragement instead. These all carried me through, the inspiring example, the advice, and the listening. Thank you Dr. Chochezi! (Tanya K.)

Testimony 3:

Over the last 20 years, I have had the privilege of working with Dr. Chochezi. During that process, she helped me complete my master's degree and my PhD. She assisted with subject matter clarifications, organization of ideas and language use. She was a very effective coach. (Angie E.)

Reference

Schuman, R. (2014, August 1). *The only thing worse than getting a Ph.d. in today's academic job market*. Slate Magazine. Retrieved July 10, 2022, from https://slate.com/human-interest/2014/08/abds-all-but-dissertation-ph-d-candidates-who-cant-quite-finish.html

ABOUT THE AUTHOR

Dr. V. S. Chochezi earned a master's degree in communication studies and an Ed.D. in educational leadership and management. She has been assisting others through the process in pursuit of advanced degrees through the years. She is a community college professor committed to student success.

www.ingramcontent.com/pod-product-compliance
Lightning Source LLC
LaVergne TN
LVHW052109160826
845678LV00015B/3455

* 9 7 9 8 8 4 0 2 1 8 9 4 5 *